Yes You Can Help But Not That Way!

The very short book for those who have loved ones suffering from depression and don't know what to do or what not to do to help them

by

Jeff Johnston

© 2019 Jeff Johnston

Hello:

On September 11, 2011, I was released from the secured ninth floor of what is now the Novant Health Presbyterian Medical Center, after spending two weeks in lock down under psychiatric supervision for suicidal tendencies.

I was diagnosed with Clinical Depression, Mood Swings, and suffered severe Anxiety Attacks. I was placed on a cocktail of Antidepressants', Xanax and Trazodone, and sent back into the "real" world...a world that had changed for me overnight. I was a zombie.

Over the next eight years, I would see Psychologists and Psychiatrists and be in therapy, constantly upgrading my medications, and trying to rebuild my "new" life, which honestly I had to fight to even care about.

I would work myself completely off my medication and then relapse...ending up in the same hospital on the same floor for a second time in July of 2014, after an attempted drug overdose.

Though over the last few years there has been more attention on Depression mainly due to celebrity suicides, there are many loved ones: parents, spouses, children, friends, and a whole society, that is not prepared to "help" the one they love.

Maybe this book will help. That is my intention.

Jeff Johnston   February 10, 2019

For Briana, Isabell and Payton

My children's children

Never be afraid to ask for help…

"Having depression and wanting to die is like being in a tall burning building and jumping out the window.

You don't want to jump… but you definitely don't want to burn to death."

Unknown Author

CHAPTER 1

It doesn't matter what the "is" is, when I have an issue.

I HAVE AN ISSUE!

I have an issue even if YOU do not understand or see what I see.

CHAPTER 2

Tough Love does not help or work.

I'd rather pull the trigger.

CHAPTER 3

If you never ever say

"Pull yourself up by your bootstraps",

you will be helping me.

CHAPTER 4

If you never ever say
"Just get over it",
you will be helping me.

CHAPTER 5

If I am seeing a therapist, you may ask me how we are getting along and do I feel like they are helping but never ever say,

"You are wasting your time and money."

CHAPTER 6

Never ever take me by the shoulders and shake me while yelling your sound advice to me.

Not good at all.

No, not good at all.

CHAPTER 7

When I am in a depression event please do not talk to me and ask me questions.

Silence is golden until this passes and I can let you know when that time comes.

CHAPTER 8

Ask me to be involved but don't get upset when I decline.

Leaving my bedroom much less my house can be an astronomical event for me.

CHAPTER 9

If I am curled up in a corner or fall down in the park on a walk with you and roll up in a ball crying, don't panic, just remain calm, speak softly and don't worry.

CHAPTER 10

The more I can talk about what is going on inside of me to someone the better.

But please do not freak out with what I say is in my head or

JUDGE ME.

I may not be willing to speak again.

CHAPTER 11

Suggest the Sedona Method to me.

What is that?

Find out.

CHAPTER 12

If you ask me to go somewhere and you tell me it's XYZ and I go and it's really ABC, be prepared for me to not do well.

I do not trust myself most places and would rather have an "event" in the privacy of my own home.

I have convinced myself to try XYZ and when you change the venue on me…WHOA!

CHAPTER 13

Loud noises and unexpected sounds can at times set me off.

CHAPTER 14

The coming of the dark night can set me off.

It makes me uneasy.

It makes me scared.

CHAPTER 15

I think it's normal to think about killing myself every day.

This may be what I am thinking when you ask "Are you okay?", and of course I say "yes."

CHAPTER 16

If you would like to sit with me while I blubber incoherently like a baby during an "event", that would be nice.

Please do not interrogate me.

That would not be nice.

CHAPTER 17

I do not want to be around other people but I do not want to be left alone.

Just being in the other room where I can hear you is helpful.

CHAPTER 18

When I am having a "depression event", responsibilities such as spouse, children, job, etc., mean nothing to me.

Please do not pressure me by using these devices.

CHAPTER 19

There are times when something "small" happens and I go off the deep end.

What you do not realize is that I have already had a series of "small" events that day and have been able to move forward.

Then this next thing makes the "load" I am carrying just too heavy, and I lose it.

CHAPTER 20

Ask me if I am familiar with Dr. Joe Dispenza and his teachings.

Who is he?

Find out.

AFTERWORD

On September 26, 2018, I was introduced to Dr. Joe Dispenza via two YouTube videos. What I heard made more sense to me than any other thing I had tried. I started his meditations and using his methods and ideas to become a "new me."

As of today, February 10, 2019, I have not had an Anxiety Attack or a Depression Event, since that introduction. From the time of being released from the hospital on September 11, 2011, I have never been able to go one week without either. Until now.

Two weeks ago I started taking only 20mg of Prosaic daily. That is all.

My objective is to be off medications completely.

This is my plan.

I AM NOT A DOCTOR.

I am a survivor.

I wish you everlasting love and patience in helping with your loved ones. I know it is difficult to understand what they are going through and I thank you for trying.

I hope I have helped even a little.

"I am in control of my mind. My mind controls my body. I am present."

"Meditation opens the door between the conscious and subconscious minds. We meditate to enter the operating system of the subconscious, where all of those unwanted habits and behaviors reside, and change them to more productive modes to support us in our lives."

Dr. Joe Dispenza,

Breaking the Habit of Being Yourself: How to Lose Your Mind and Create a New One

Other Books by Jeff Johnston

PoextS Year Seven

PoextS and Pics: First Edition

So Far…Compilation

PoextS Year Six

The Purple Diamond Queen

PoextS Year Five

PoextS Year Four

it's not black or white

PoextS Year Three

PoextS Year Two

PoextS Year One

So Far…Book 3

So Far…Book 2

So Far…Book 1

……………………………………………………………………

PoextS.com

JeffJohnstonPoet.com

Facebook…poexts

Twitter…@poexts

Instagram…poexts_by_jeff

Made in the USA
San Bernardino, CA
20 February 2019